CONTENTS

Piano Arrangements By: PAUL McKIBBINS

ALL THE LIVELONG DAY
("I Hear America Singing" - Walt Whitman)

from the Musical "Working"

Music and Additional Lyrics by
STEPHEN SCHWARTZ

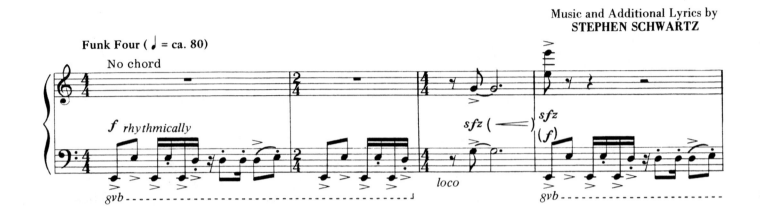

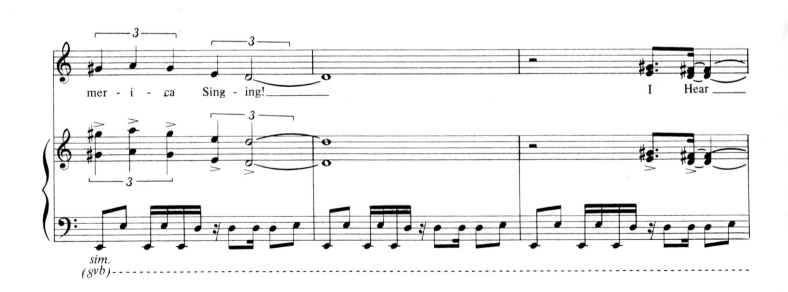

6

LOVIN' AL

from the Musical "Working"

Music and Lyrics by
MICKI GRANT

Lovin' Al - 8

14

Lovin' Al - 8

15

Lovin' Al - 8

THE MASON

From the Musical "Working"

Music and Lyrics by
CRAIG CARNELIA

18

The Mason - 4

20

The Mason - 4

NEAT TO BE A NEWSBOY

from the Musical "Working"

Music and Lyrics by
STEPHEN SCHWARTZ

22

Neat To Be A Newsboy - 6

NOBODY TELLS ME HOW

from the Musical "Working"

Lyrics by **SUSAN BIRKENHEAD**
Music by **MARY RODGERS**

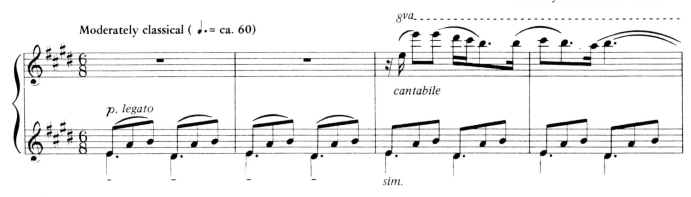

class-room was al-ways a show-case; In those days, we did it our-

28

selves. With col - or - ful pic - tures and charts on the wall, A

snow - man in Win - ter, A pump - kin in Fall, And all my sup - plies were in

neat lit - tle piles on the shelves. My

chil - dren were al - ways ex - am - ples, When the Prin - ci - pal came they would

Nobody Tells Me How - 8

rise.   If   I   left   the   room   for   a   min - ute   or   two,   They

cresc.

al - ways   found   some-thing   "con-struc - tive"   to do,   And   ev - 'ry - one   sat   in   their

cresc.

decresc.   *mp*

plac - es   ac-cord - ing   to   size.   But

decresc.

kids   don't   know   how   to   be - have   an - y - more: Ask   them   to   rise   and   they'll

mp

ask you "What for?" They write on the walls and they sit on the floor. It's

called "In - for-mal - i - ty" now. They want me to teach in a

class - room like that, but No - bod - y tells me how! ____

I made a big thing a - bout spell - ing— but they

Who has the time be-tween weav - ing and clay? The words they can spell I'm em-

bar - rassed to say. They're "Free to ex-press them - selves" now. The

way I've been teach - ing for for - ty - one years is no long - er "Ef - fec - tive" or

so it ap-pears... Well, dam-mit, it worked for me then, So what's wrong with it

now? _____ They say I'm sup-posed to "Keep

rit. **Broadly** *cresc.*

up with the times," but No-bod-y ev-er tells me

ff

34

Nobody Tells Me How - 8

UN MEJOR DIA VENDRA

from the Musical "Working"

Lyrics by **GRACIELA DANIELE** and **MATT LANDERS**
Music by **JAMES TAYLOR**

38

Un Mejor Dia Vendra - 4

JUST A HOUSEWIFE

From the Musical "Working"

Music and Lyrics by
CRAIG CARNELIA

Just A Housewife - 8

44

Just A Housewife - 8

MILLWORK

from the Musical "Working"

Music and Lyrics by
JAMES TAYLOR

54

rest of my life.

IF I COULD'VE BEEN

from the musical "Working"

Music and Lyrics by
MICKI GRANT

If I Could've Been - 4

58

If I Could've Been - 4

If I Could've Been - 4

JOE

From the Musical "Working"

Music and Lyrics by
CRAIG CARNELIA

(spoken) When I retired, the first two years I was downhearted. I had no place to go, nothin' to do. But then I gave myself a good goin'-over. "Joe," I said, "you can't sit at home like that and waste your time. You got to get out and do things."
Well, the day goes pretty fast for me now. I don't daydream at all. I just think o' somethin', and I forget it. That day-dreamin', it don't do you no good.
Keep busy, keep movin', that's the trick.

62

Joe - 10

Joe - 10

prayed. *The "Big Dipper" they called it.* We could hard - ly walk as we left the car, so we stag - gered down for a can - dy bar. Then we sat and laughed in the pen - ny ar - cade.

At six— o-'clock you watch— the news. *Them politicians get you so mad, you throw your slippers at the set.*

You cook— some franks, no big— to-do's. *Most nights you lay around, you straighten up, maybe you call your daughter.*

You watch— a game. You take— a snooze. *But then there's Sunday. Sunday's different.*

You change— your shirt, and shine your shoes, *'Cause you're goin' around the block to the tavern.*

66

Joe - 10

Joe - 10

I can hear_ her say: *"Joe!"*

They drive_ you home from 'round_ the block.

You take_ your cash out of__ your sock.

Joe - 10

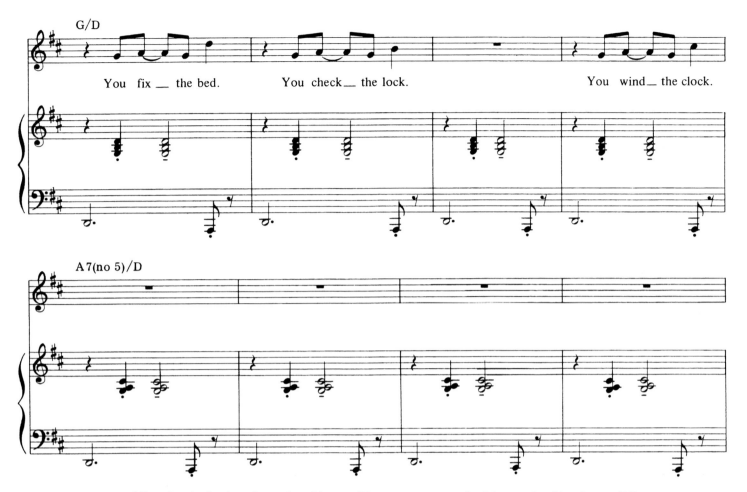

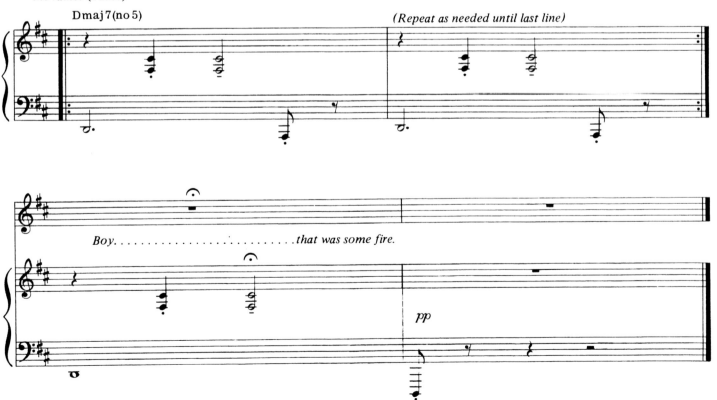

When I retired a lot o' people told me: "Joe, you got your health, you shouldna done it." But it was too late. I don't know why I retired. It's just a habit, I guess.

But I got no regrets. I keep busy, keep travelin'. I go to fires every once in awhile. That big fire we had on Milwaukee Avenue about 3 months ago, I was there. I was surprised that the smoke was comin' out there heavy as hell, but you don't see no flames, you know. (Pause) They musta had about thirty units there. (Pause) You. . .you get the news over the radio. (Pause)

Joe - 10

IT'S AN ART

from the Musical "Working"

Music and Lyrics by
STEPHEN SCHWARTZ

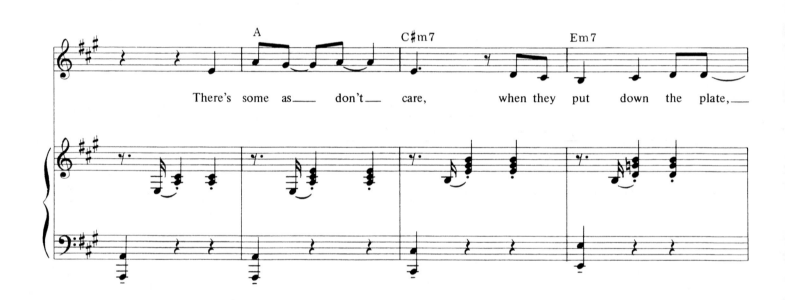

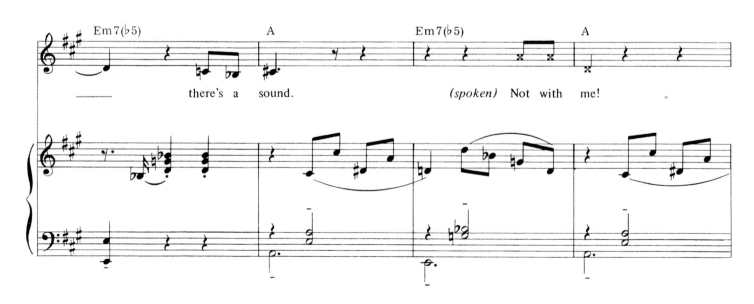

72

It's An Art - 14

That's what makes it an art!

I re-mem-ber one day, as I do now and then, I had— shakes.— *(spoken)* Down I went!

(sung) There with my tray—— full of sev-en prime—

It's An Art - 14

82

It's An Art - 14

but I'm not just a wait-ress,

I'm a one _____ wo - man _____ show. _____

BROTHER TRUCKER

from the Musical "Working"

Music and Lyrics by
JAMES TAYLOR

Brother Trucker - 8

86

*Small notes denote vocal harmony.

Brother Trucker - 8

90

Brother Trucker - 8

FATHERS AND SONS

from the Musical "Working"

Music and Lyrics by
STEPHEN SCHWARTZ

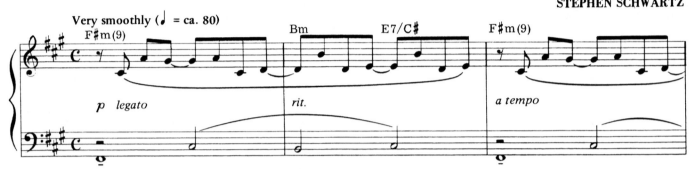

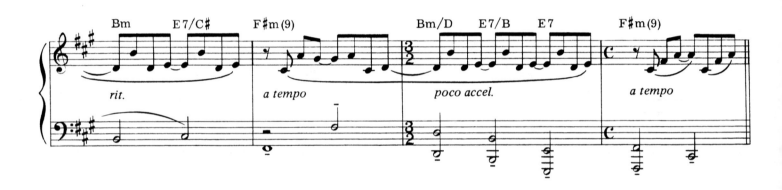

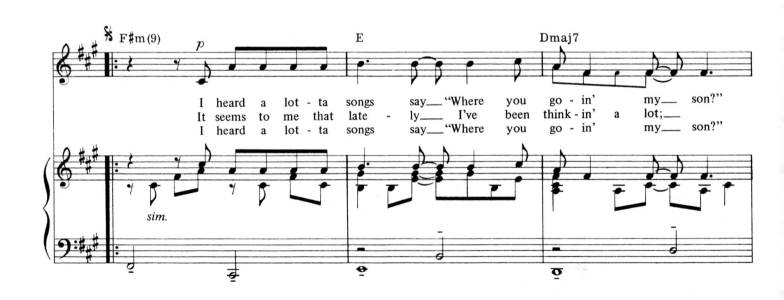

I heard a lot - ta songs say __ "Where you go - in' my __ son?"
It seems to me that late - ly __ I've been think - in' a lot; __
I heard a lot - ta songs say __ "Where you go - in' my __ son?"

96

Fathers And Sons - 6

CLEANIN' WOMEN

from the Musical "Working"

Music and Lyrics by
MICKI GRANT

Ma - ma worked just like her Ma - ma be - fore____ her Do -

100

Cleanin' Women - 9

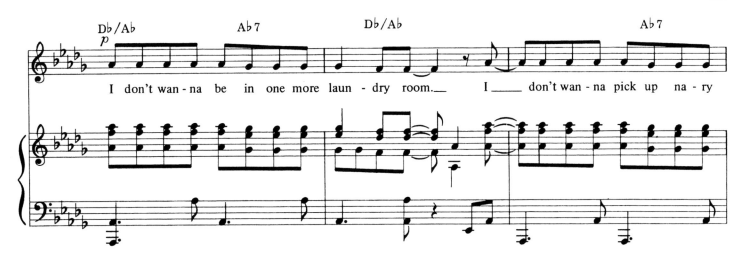

Cleanin' Women - 9

SOMETHING TO POINT TO

From the Musical "Working"

Music and Lyrics by
CRAIG CARNELIA

See that build-ing; — I was the one — who did the de-sign. — I was the one — who draft-ed the plans, — ev-'ry de-tail — and ev-'ry line. — See that — build-ing; — I ran the crane — that lift-ed the beams. — I was the guy — who

Something To Point To - 7

Something To Point To - 7

Something To Point To - 7